JOAN TOWER

ASCENT

for Organ

AMP 8134

First Printing: June 1999

ISBN 0–7935–8775–1

Associated Music Publishers, Inc.

DISTRIBUTED BY

 HAL•LEONARD®
CORPORATION

7777 W. BLUEMOUND RD. P.O. BOX 13819 MILWAUKEE, WI 53213

PROGRAM NOTE

Ascent was commissioned by the American Guild of Organists and is dedicated to Cherry Rhodes, who gave its premiere performance as part of the AGO National Convention in 1996.

When I was approached to write this piece, I decided to keep the length deliberately brief (about ten minutes) mainly because this was the first time I had ever written music for the organ. The title *Ascent* is quite direct in its description of the upward-moving scales in the piece, which form the central thematic action.

I would like to thank Ms. Rhodes for her invaluable help in determining registrations.

—JOAN TOWER

*Ascent was first performed on July 7, 1996 by Cherry Rhodes
at St. Ignatius Loyola Church, New York City*

duration: ca. 10 minutes

Suggested Registrations:

◆**1**
Pedal:	foundations 16' through mixture, bassoon 16'
Great:	foundations 16' through mixture, cornet, reeds 16', 8', 4'
Positive:	foundations 8' through 2', trumpet 8', cromorne 8'
Swell:	foundations 8' through mixtures, cornet, reeds 16', 8', 4'
Couplers:	Great and Swell to Pedal, Positve and Swell to Great

◆**2** = ◆**1** plus:
Positive:	mixture, cornet
Bombarde (IV):	reeds 16', 8', trompette en chamade 8' (if it blends)
Couplers:	Bombarde to Great

◆**3**
Pedal:	same as ◆**2**
Great:	flute 8', gemshorn or string 8'
Positive:	flute 8', 1⅓'
Swell:	flute 8', salicional 8'
Bombarde (IV):	harmonic flute 8'
Couplers:	Great and Swell to Pedal, Swell to Great

◆**4**
Pedal:	soft 16's
Great:	foundations 8', flute 4'
Positive:	foundations 8'
Swell:	foundations 8', 4', oboe 8'
Couplers:	Great and Swell to Pedal, Swell to Great

◆**5** = ◆**4** plus: Swell trumpet 8'

◆**6**
Pedal:	foundations 16', principal 8'
Great:	foundations 8', 4', 2 2/3', 2'
Positive:	foundations 8', 4', 2 2/3', 2', trumpet 8'
Swell:	foundations 8', 4', light reed 16', reeds 8'
Couplers:	Great and Swell to Pedal, Positive and Swell to Great

◆**7** = ◆**6** plus: cornets and Great trumpet 8'

◆**8**
Pedal:	principal 8', trumpet 8'
Great:	foundations 8' through mixtures, cornet, reeds 8', 4'
Positive:	foundations 8' through mixtures, cornet, trumpet 8'
Swell:	foundations 8' through mixtures, cornet, reeds 8', light reed 16'
Couplers:	Swell to Pedal, Positive and Swell to Great

◆**9** = ◆**8** except for Pedal
Pedal:	foundations 32' through 4'
Bombarde (IV):	(optional) reed 16', en chamade reeds 8', 4'

◆**10** = ◆**9** plus:
Pedal:	mixture, reeds 16', 8'
Great:	principal 16'
Swell:	reeds 16', 4'
Coupler:	Great to Pedal

◆**11**
Pedal:	foundations 32' through mixture, bassoon 16'
Great:	foundations 8' through mixtures, cornet, reeds 16', 8', 4'
Positive:	foundations 8' through mixtures, cornet, reeds 8'
Swell:	foundations 8' through mixtures, cornet, reeds 16', 8', 4'
Couplers:	Swell to Pedal, Positive and Swell to Great, Swell to Positive

◆**12** = ◆**11** minus:
Great:	high mixture, reed 16'
Swell:	mixture, heavy reed 8', reed 4'

◆**13** = ◆**12** plus:
Pedal:	reed 32'
Great:	high mixture, reed 16'
Bombarde (IV):	reed 16', en chamade 4'
Coupler:	Bombarde to Great

◆**14**
Great:	flutes 8'
Positive:	flute 8'
Swell:	flute 8'
Bombarde (IV):	harmonic flute 8'
Coupler:	Swell to Great

Manual Pistons
Swell ④:	foundations 8', oboe 8' or salicional 8', flutes 8', 4'
Swell ⑤:	Swell ④ plus principal 8'
Great ③:	foundations 8', flute 4'
Pedal ①:	soft 16's

Whenever the term "flute" is used, choose the kind that sounds best for the passage and instrument.

◇ = general piston
○ = manual piston

commissioned by the American Guild of Organists
dedicated to Cherry Rhodes

ASCENT

Joan Tower
edited by Cherry Rhodes

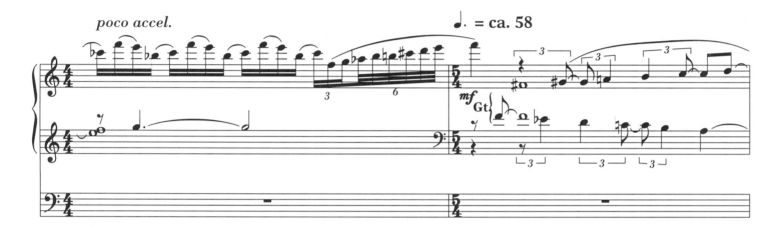

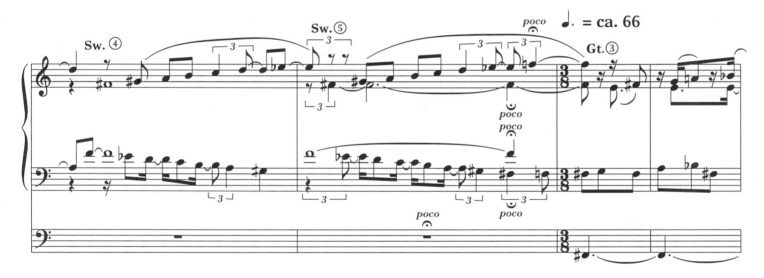

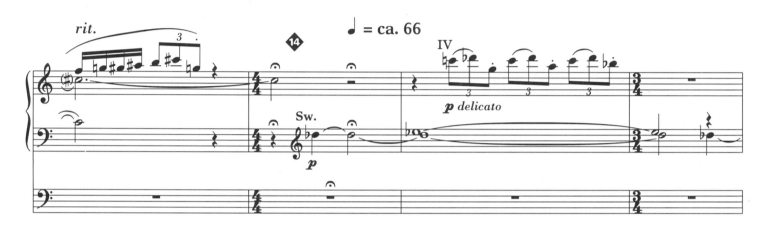

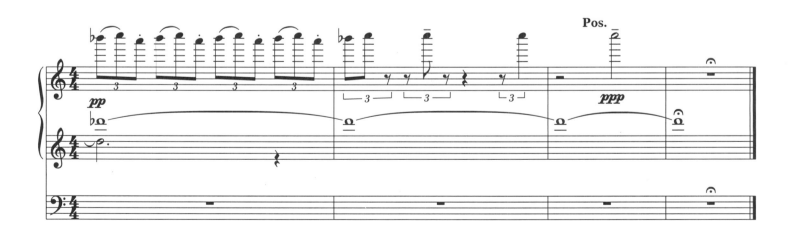